Real Estate Inve

Real Estate Investing Through Tax Liens and Deeds

---※---

The Beginner's Guide to Earning a

Sustainable Passive Income While

Reducing Risks (Traditional Buy and

Hold Doesn't Work Anymore)

---※---

Phil C. Senior

Bluesource And Friends

This book is brought to you by Bluesource And Friends, a happy book publishing company.

Our motto is **"Happiness Within Pages"**

We promise to deliver amazing value to readers with our books.

We also appreciate honest book reviews from our readers.

Connect with us on our Facebook page www.facebook.com/bluesourceandfriends and stay tuned to our latest book promotions and free giveaways.

Real Estate Investing Through AirBNB Rental Arbitrage:

The Beginner's Guide To Earning Sustainable A Passive Income Without **Owning Any Property** (Traditional Buy & Hold Doesn't Work Anymore)

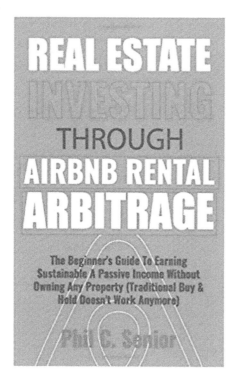

Buy now on Amazon.com today!

Don't forget to claim your FREE books!

Brain Teasers:

https://tinyurl.com/karenbrainteasers

Harry Potter Trivia:

https://tinyurl.com/wizardworldtrivia

Sherlock Puzzle Book (Volume 2)

https://tinyurl.com/Sherlockpuzzlebook2

Also check out our best seller book

"67 Lateral Thinking Puzzles"

https://tinyurl.com/thinkingandriddles

irrespective of if it is done electronically or in print. This extends to creating a secondary or tertiary copy of the work or a recorded copy, and is only allowed with express written consent from the Publisher. All additional rights reserved.

The information in the following pages is broadly considered to be a truthful and accurate account of facts. As such, any inattention, use, or misuse of the information in question by the reader will render any resulting actions solely under their purview. There are no scenarios in which the publisher nor the original author of this work can be in any fashion deemed liable for any hardship or damages that may befall them after undertaking information described herein.

Additionally, the information in the following pages is intended for informational purposes only and should thus be thought of as universal. As befitting to its nature, it is presented without assurance regarding its prolonged validity or interim quality. Trademarks that are mentioned are done without written consent and can in no way be considered an endorsement from the trademark holder.

Table of Contents

1. You will be unlikely to get a certain property out of the process
2. Understand your jurisdiction
3. Tax investing is an active process
4. You can indirectly buy tax liens via privately held funds
5. Interest rates may surprise you
6. Consider working with a tax lien professional
7. Tax liens are prone to exposure
8. Learn as much as you can about tax lien investing

Chapter 3: Finding Profitable Tax Liens

Strategies

1. Buy-and-Hold Strategy
2. The Assignment Strategy
3. The Foreclosure Strategy

Identifying Profitable Tax Liens

Procedure

Chapter 4: Property Evaluation, Bidding, and Auction

Tax Lien Certificate Buying Procedures

Count the costs

Verify the lien

Examine and inspect the property

Read the local laws

Procedures for Identifying Tax Lien Properties

How to Bid on a Tax Lien Property

1. Use the bid-down approach.

2. Bid down on the ownership.

3. Premium Bidding

4. Random Selection

5. Off-the-Shelf Purchase

Crucial Points to Know About Tax Lien Bidding

More than just interest rates

Lien investing requires patience and cash.

Buy tax liens closer to your home.

You are not necessarily investing in real estate.

Chapter 5: Pitfalls and Risks of Tax Lien Investing

Chapter 6: Investing in Tax Deeds

1. Research the property before auction day

2. Pay auction deposits and fees

3. Bid and participate at the auction

4. Understand the terminology

5. Buy the tax deed after the auction

6. Profit with tax deeds

Conclusion

Introduction

Congratulations on getting this book, and thank you for doing so!

The following chapters will discuss safer ways to invest in the real estate sector but without the stresses of landlords or the risks of the financial markets. Instruments such as property tax liens and tax deeds provide alternative ways of investing in real estate without all the headache and high cost involved.

Generally, when you invest in tax liens and tax deeds, you are investing in properties where their owners have unpaid taxes and are therefore delinquent. As an investor, you earn interest and profit from tax liens and sometimes even penalty fees. In some instances, you are able to acquire a property at prices that are way below market rates through tax deeds and tax liens.

How Do Tax Deeds and Liens Work?

Property owners are sometimes unable to pay their taxes to local authorities. In some cases, they may owe debts to the federal government. In cases where a property owner is delinquent, the authorities, whether county or city, have the power to foreclose a property and sell it or place a lien on it in order to recover taxes owed.

Municipal or county authorities can place a tax lien on a home when the owner fails to pay the taxes they owe. This lien is then sold to willing buyers. A buyer will pay the money that they ask for, and he or she will then have legal rights to request the owner to repay the money with interest.

Tax Liens in the USA

Investing in tax lien certificates across the United States has been going on for the past 200 years. There are individuals who simply won't meet their tax obligations or are completely unable to pay property taxes.

Governments need this money in order to provide services to the community. Local and county authorities use funds received from property taxes to pay the police, fund schools, local courts, fire departments, road maintenance, and county workers. When authorities sell tax lien certificates, they are essentially seeking funds that are due to them from delinquent property owners.

The act of selling tax lien certificates and tax deeds enables authorities to obtain the funds necessary to provide citizens with the services they deserve. It is investors who buy these tax liens and tax deeds. When they do, they provide governments with the money they need. In return, they gain rights to the property as well as interests due when the property is eventually sold. Should the owner completely fail to pay the taxes and penalties, then a tax lien investor will gain the right to foreclose the property.

Opportunities for Small Investors

If you are looking for ways to make a passive and steady income devoid of all the risks and stresses of other investment vehicles, then you should how to invest in tax liens. As it is right now, there are plenty of opportunities out there for investors just like you. There are plenty of properties out there that large investors and banks will never buy.

This kind of investment opportunity is suitable for conservative investors who prefer profitable ventures without any significant risks. It is crucial that you learn more about tax lien certificates investing and how to go about the process. Tax lien and deed certificates investing are lucrative investment

16

opportunities that allow you to invest your money with the government and receive a check that you can cash out.

The best part is that you do not need large sums of money to invest in tax deeds. People invest as little as $50 and $100, while others choose to invest larger amounts. You can buy tax lien certificates and then sell them to others for a profit.

Chapter 1: Investing in Tax Lien and Deed Certificates

One of the most lucrative ways of investing your money is doing so in the real estate sector. However, you do not need hundreds of thousands of dollars, and neither do you have to buy property. There are better ways of investing in the real estate sector and receive a passive, stress-free, and sustainable income. This is through tax liens and tax deeds.

What Is a Tax Lien?

A tax lien is basically a lien that is imposed on a property by local authorities when taxes due on that property are not paid. The law allows a tax lien to be imposed on a specific property—either when taxes are unpaid on the property or when other taxes such as income taxes remain unpaid.

18

A lien is simply a right to take possession of a person's belonging, usually property, until any debts that they owe is paid. In brief terms, we can say that a tax lien is basically a claim against a property.

What Is a Tax Deed?

On the other hand, a tax deed can be defined as a legal document that basically awards the ownership of a property to a government body in the event where the owner fails to pay any taxes that they owe.

How Do Tax Liens and Tax Deeds Work?

As already established, tax deed and tax lien investing involve the purchase of property with unpaid property taxes. As an investor, you will benefit from these real estate investment vehicles through interest payments and sometimes through penalties. In some cases, as an investor, you will be able to acquire some of the properties at prices that are far below market rates.

If a homeowner fails to pay property taxes, he or she becomes delinquent, and the local authorities can choose to either foreclose the property or place a lien on the home. When a tax lien is placed on a home or another property, the lien will be sold off to investors at a certain price, and the owner will collect premiums and interests once the taxes owed are resolved.

Property owners are actually provided some time to come up with the taxes they owe the government. Some people do get 3 months, while others do get more time—and in some cases, they even get 2 years. This time depends on the state laws, among other factors. All this time, the taxes are accruing interest. An investor who holds a lien will be entitled to receive the interests on the amount invested. They would also be entitled to any penalties should the payments be late, and so on.

As soon as the entire debt is paid or resolved, investors will get paid for their investment as well as for all other costs and penalties.

Deed Certificates

Sometimes, city and county authorities use deed certificates rather than tax liens. In such cases, the property is often auctioned, and investors get to bid for it. A winning bidder could easily end up with the title to a particular property within 24 hours of the auction.

However, most property owners are given time to come up with the money owed. This is a redemption period that lasts no more than a couple of months. During this redemption period, interests and penalties will accrue to which the investor is entitled. Should the owner fail to pay the taxes, then the investor will be allowed to foreclose the property.

There is a difference between investing in deed certificates and tax lien certificates. When you invest in tax liens, you are purchasing the certificates in order to earn interests and, in some cases, penalties. With deed certificates, your main purpose of investing is to eventually acquire a property at a very low price through what is known as a "tax foreclosure" on a property. States get to choose whether to use tax liens or tax deeds.

Basics of Tax Lien Investing

One of the reasons why tax liens are the preferred investment vehicle for numerous investors is because of higher than average interest rates with almost zero risk. You can expect to receive at least a 16% return on your investment, and in some instances, you can earn up to 36% interest rate. Investors also get to receive penalty fees in some instances, which will increase their income greatly.

Property owners do get a grace period within which to sort out their delinquencies. In case this time period expires, then a certain interest will be charged by the city, municipality or other relevant authority. When you invest your money in a tax lien, your funds will be used in place of those of the delinquent property owner. This is, in essence, paying for his or her indebtedness.

As soon as you become the official holder of a certificate, you will have the right to receive all interests and penalties accruing until the time when the property owner will redeem their property. In order for the owner to redeem their property, he or she will first have to clear all the costs, fees, and penalties.

For instance, let us assume that a property owner owes $2,000 on their property taxes. In this case, there is a $40 penalty that is due every 6 months as

well as a 15% interest charged on the amount owed.
You buy the tax lien certificate for this property and
hold onto it for 9 months, after which the owner
finally pays off all of his dues.

Sample earnings

Total amount you invested

$2,000

---

9 months of interest at 15%

$225

Penalty charges (2 X 40)

$80

Total amount received at redemption

$2,305

Profit earned within the period

$305

Effective annual yield earned

20.3%

In the example above, you will earn a total of $2,305 once the owner repays their debts in full. This is the amount that you earn in just 9 months. You will find tax lien certificates on almost all kinds of properties within US states that apply this system. Very few other investment opportunities offer such lucrative returns. Stock markets are very volatile and wrought with risks. Banks and funds offer very low returns on savings and investments. Not even gold is this lucrative. Tax liens, on the other hand, are lucrative, easy to invest in, offer excellent returns, and have very little risk.

Chapter 2: Why Invest in Tax Liens?

There are numerous reasons why you should invest in tax liens. However, the best reason of all is that you get a win-win situation. This means that, no matter what the outcome will be, you will always be a winner with tax liens.

Imagine playing heads or tails by tossing a coin. Traditionally, the rules would be: If heads, I win; if tails I lose. However, when investing in tax liens, the rules would become: If heads, I win; if tails, I win *even more*. This is the very essence of risk management in investing: If the owner pays up, then I get paid fantastic interest returns. If the owner doesn't pay up, I get paid with a property.

Reasons to Invest in Tax Liens

There are numerous reasons why you should invest your money in tax liens rather than other investment vehicles. One of the main reasons is that it is among the safest and most reliable forms of investment that you can find out there. The reason has to do with taxes. It has often been said that there two things that are inevitable in life: These are taxes and death. Taxes levied on a property have to be paid. It is this reason why tax lien investing is so secure. Here are some more reasons why you should invest in tax lien certificates.

High Returns and Low Risks

Basically, it is municipalities and county authorities who impose tax liens on properties. They are the ones who issue the certificates and deeds in order to collect any unpaid property taxes. These deeds and certificates are closely monitored, and there is very little chance for fraud. This makes them very safe as an investment option.

28

Another reason is that tax liens refer to real, tangible investments and not mere paper. Should a delinquent property owner fail to pay back taxes, then their property could be sold off to recover the property taxes due. This makes them extremely motivated to pay their taxes and interests as well.

When it comes to ranking of liens, tax liens are ranked up there with other government liens. They are considered to be senior liens and rank above all other liens. This means that they must be paid first. This means that, as an investor, your investment will be given a priority and will definitely be paid.

You also enjoy solid and secured interests. Once the interest rate is set at the onset, there will be no further negotiations, and the rates and interests will have to be paid on time and in full. Again, in case the property owner fails to pay their taxes, then their property may be forfeited and foreclosed. No matter how you look at it, you will always emerge the winner.

When you buy a tax lien certificate, you will essentially be spending only a modest amount to secure an entire property. The amount received by the government, whether it's local or county, is only a fraction of the total value of the home. However, the leverage is pretty high—and that is why in 99% of the time, homeowners often pay their taxes and all interests and penalties.

Another excellent reason to invest in tax liens is not just for the healthy profits that you will make from interest and penalty payments, but you will also be supporting communities in the given locality. Tax liens net authorities over $20 billion each year, which is used to fund school programs, pay the police, provide essential infrastructure, and so much more.

When homeowners fail to pay their property taxes, then cities and counties are denied funds which they need to maintain parks, fund the fire departments, and keep hospitals running. Your funds go a long way in supporting not just the community, but also provide delinquent property owners the time they need to find money to pay their back taxes whilst holding on to their properties.

Finally, it is crucial to learn that most properties never get forfeited. Properties receive protection from foreclosure from owners, mortgage holders, and family and friends. As such, tax lien investing remains largely an excellent choice for investors, especially small investors seeking a safe and secure investment opportunity.

Tips and Advice on Tax Lien Investing

Before investing in tax liens, there are a couple of things you need to learn. A tax lien certificate is generally considered to be a safe and profitable investment vehicle that is collateralized and can be used to balance your portfolio. Here are some tips and friendly advice to help guide you along.

1. You will be unlikely to get a certain property out of the process

Basically, you do not invest in tax liens with the hopes or expectations of getting a house out of it at a throwaway price. About 98% of all property owners eventually pay their back taxes and keep their homes without any foreclosures. Even after a tax foreclosure begins, most property owners get to redeem their homes. Only about 0.5% may end up losing their homes. When foreclosures do actually occur, it does so mostly on vacant lots and undeveloped real estate.

2. Understand your jurisdiction

If you wish to purchase tax liens in a particular county or municipality, then you need to understand exactly how the process works. Basically, you will need to learn how the sale or auction process works and if there is a possibility of making any money through the process.

Years back, counties used to fret at the thought of selling tax liens and deeds. It was a chore that was not always necessary successful. However, developments in the digital world and the popularity of the internet and social media have seen increased activity in property tax participation as they have made the process more visible and easily accessible.

3. Tax investing is an active process

Some investors view tax lien investing as akin to investing in certificates of deposit (CDs). This is because CDs are generally short-term instruments that are considered relatively safe.

However, the two are quite different in certain aspects. For instance, CDs require no action once you own them, while tax liens are pretty active. You will be expected to check on when tax liens are to be redeemed regularly, and there is also some management and servicing of these liens. Therefore, always keep this in mind.

4. You can indirectly buy tax liens via privately held funds

Another thing you need to keep in mind is that tax lien investing is quite a hands-on process. It is also rather time consuming. As such, you may want to consider investing via a private fund. There are plenty of private funds as well as tax lien servicers who are willing to do the hard work on your behalf. If you have plenty of funds to invest in tax liens, then engaging a servicer will be of great help to you.

5. Interest rates may surprise you

There are laws in place across each jurisdiction that governs the rate of interest charged on tax liens. In some states, this can be as high as 1.5% per month. In Florida, for instance, the highest interest rate that can be charged is 18%. Other states such as Iowa charge upwards of 2% per month on unpaid balances. Even then, you are likely to find out that most states have structures in place, which means that you are rarely likely to earn more than 9%. Whenever you want to invest in tax liens, focus on investing from 3% to 7% of the value of the property.

6. Consider working with a tax lien professional

Are you new to the game and without a lot of time on your hands? Sometimes, it is much easier to use the services of a professional to get things done. In the USA, over 80% of tax liens are purchased by people who are members of the National Tax Liens Association (NTLA). A lot of the members are also fund managers, which means that they are experts who know what they are doing. Therefore, if you wish to be successful, one of the pathways to follow may be investing through tax lien professionals.

7. Tax liens are prone to exposure

While tax liens are relatively safe investment vehicles, they are not necessarily safe from exposure. According to experts, tax liens are not affected by the markets and hence are very predictable and considered largely safe. However, this safety can be affected by rising interest rates in the housing sector. When home prices begin to rise, homeowners are able to sell their homes faster, which will make things tougher for tax lien investors. The reverse is true when there is little activity in the housing sector because tax liens will perform quite well. Also, do not rush to purchase a house whose value is really low, as this will cause you to miss out on interests and lose part of your principle, since no-one may be interested in it.

8. Learn as much as you can about tax lien investing

It is advisable that you learn as much as possible about tax lien investing. For instance, you could participate in investor courses offered by the NTLA, the national body for professional tax liens investors. Their courses prepare you for the practical aspects of investing in liens, and all the necessary knowledge you

36

need to avoid pitfalls and invest smartly. It is also advisable to learn about the rules and regulations governing auctions, and the laws in place that affect tax liens.

Chapter 3: Finding Profitable Tax Liens

As an investor, you want to get the best return on your investment. As such, it is crucial to identify which are the most profitable tax liens available. In recent years, there has been growing interest in tax lien investing, and for very good reasons. For starters, you can expect to receive very good rates for your investment, and also because there is very little risk involved.

If you are informed about how the process works and all other procedures, this will enable you to avoid making mistakes or costly errors. A property with a lien placed on it cannot be sold or re-financed until all taxes owed are repaid and the lien removed. As an investor, you want to find the most profitable liens in the market. Reports indicate there are over $14 billion in unpaid property taxes across the US, and about

38

30% of this amount is usually sold off to investors like you.

Local authorities prefer selling tax lien certificates as these bring in instant cash, which they then use to provide services to residents and execute their other obligations. Before investing your funds in a tax lien, you should choose the best strategy that fits your investment aims.

Strategies

There are several strategies that you can choose from. These include the Buy-and-Hold Strategy, Foreclosure Strategy, and Assignment Strategy. The Buy-and-Hold Strategy is best applied in states that offer the best interest rates. The Assignment Strategy is suitable for investors who wish to enter and exit a trade quickly without their money being held for lengthy periods of time, while Foreclosure Strategy will see a property sold off.

1. Buy-and-Hold Strategy

This strategy is best applied in states offering some of the highest interest rates in the market. You can adapt this strategy if you intend to invest in such counties, so that the interest accumulates over time. Ideally, investors often hold onto the tax lien until a property owner pays off all back taxes, or until foreclosure. For instance, the state of Florida offers interest rates of 18% on tax liens. If you invest $1,000 in tax liens for 5 years, you will earn a total of $900 in interest only.

2. The Assignment Strategy

This is a strategy that is preferred by investors who wish to invest in tax liens but do not want their money locked up for lengthy periods of time. You will find that most counties actually allow you to sell or transfer your liens to other investors, and sometimes even to the secondary markets. As an investor, you can also sell your tax liens at other platforms, which include online marketplaces such as eBay and others. The process is really easy as it has been digitalized for purposes of convenience.

3. The Foreclosure Strategy

This is a tax lien strategy that requires you to buy a property tax lien in a given county. There is usually a certain time period that has to elapse before a property can be foreclosed. For instance, in Arizona, this period is approximately 3 years, while in Florida, this process is almost imminent.

If you intend to foreclose a property, you will need to check with the tax collector's office in the respective county. The office will notify you when the process is imminent. Once the foreclosure process is complete, you will receive the deed to the property.

Identifying Profitable Tax Liens

Most states list their liens on their websites. As such, you should take the time to view the websites of different states across the US. Some of the more popular ones include Illinois, Florida, and Arizona. As it is right now, Florida happens to be among the most popular states, offering interest rates as high as 18% on tax liens. In fact, since this interest is not annualized, it can sometimes be as high as 36% per annum.

A rate of 36% is extremely attractive even without any penalties, and with penalties, you can expect to earn a really attractive income. Let's take the example of an investor who takes out a tax lien on a property in Florida at the rate of 18%. The lien is then redeemed seven months later, so you can collect your earnings and premium.

When you collect your return, you will actually receive a return of close to 62%, which is much better than an annualized return. Sometimes, there is a challenge to investors because the liens in some counties are not posted online. As such, your physical presence will be required at auctions. You will have to drive there and actually participate in the bids. Also, competition is often intense because of the attractive interest rates.

Procedure

You should first contact the tax office or registrar's office in any county, city, or municipality that you think has attractive liens. It is advisable to do some due diligence first.

Due diligence

As an investor, the first thing you need to do is due diligence on the available properties. The reason is that, in some instances, the current value of a home can be much lower than the lien. As an investor, it is advisable to assess the worth of a lien certificate by dividing the amount of the delinquent tax lien with the property's market value. This ratio should not be above 4%. If it is, then you should avoid it. Some properties sometimes have more than one lien placed on them.

Each county places a distinct number on every piece of real estate with a tax lien. It is much easier for investors to search for liens using the assigned numbers. It is easy to do this online from the comfort of your home or office computer. Each number will provide you with details about a property, including their address, the property's assessed value, and the name of the owner. It will also contain information about the property's condition, as well as any other structures within the compound.

Pay lien amount in cash

Upon purchase of a tax lien certificate, the county or municipality will expect you to pay the lien amount in full immediately. In most American states, the issuer often collects the interest amount, principal amount, and any other fees or charges. Then, he or she pays the lien certificate investor before collecting the certificate. Interest rates on liens range from 5% to almost 40%. Sometimes, investors pay a premium for the tax lien certificates. This amount is sometimes refunded, though not always.

While you are likely to receive a substantial interest rate on your investment, you really should do your homework before investing in this venture. Good understanding of the real estate market is advisable, so do your homework well before investing.

Your due diligence should include thorough research, official searches and so much more. It is actually a costly affair and can take a long while. You will need to be familiar with a property if you are to invest in a lien confidently. This will ensure that you are able to collect your money from the owner when the time comes. Also, some properties that are dilapidated or located in a tough neighborhood are not a good investment. But, you may not know this without proper due diligence.

There are properties that have suffered from some damage due to natural or environmental reasons. For instance, homes can be damaged by hazardous or chemical materials deposited in the area. Such properties are generally undesirable, and probably unsuitable for tax lien certificate investing.

Upon receiving a lien certificate, you should know what your responsibilities are. For instance, you will need to notify the property owner about the lien certificate purchase in writing. And then towards the end of the redemption period, you will need to send another reminder should payments not be received on time and in full.

Tax liens have expiration dates and do not last forever. The expiration date comes after the expiry of the redemption period. You will need to collect any unpaid monies or take some other form of action before the expiry date—otherwise, you will be unable to do so afterward. Also, should the property go into foreclosure, there is a possibility of other liens on the same property being revealed. This will likely make it difficult to acquire the title.

Large investors like hedge funds and banks have expressed an interest in tax lien investing. Such investors are able to outbid individual investors. They also drive down bids and reduce profitability. This has made it difficult for individual investors to invest profitably in tax lien certificates. Fortunately, though, there are some funds that now invest in tax lien certificates, and this opens the door for novice investors to venture into this sector.

Repayment schedules

Tax lien certificates have repayment schedules that range from 6 months to almost 3 years. Most property owners often pay lien and charges in full. However, if they are unable to do so within the stipulated period of time, you may be required to foreclose the property even though this rarely is the case.

Check the listings

Contact the local county's tax records or registrar's office, then request for all the tax lien listings available. You should also request for information on any impending auctions. These are usually available, and you will only pay the cost of printing. You can do this across a number of counties in several states. It is at this stage that you will do your due diligence.

Once you have done your due diligence, you will then proceed to select the properties that you are interested in. You should contact the relevant office and confirm a couple of things, such as the interest rates that the county will pay for the taxes owed. Sometimes, this percentage is high even though it varies from state to state. As soon as you identify a lien that you are interested in, you should proceed to the tax office and pay for the lien. Do so in cash if you can, and you will be registered as the holder of the lien of the particular home.

Make sure that you receive the tax lien certificate complete with dates and a payment receipt. You should keep these documents handy until such a time when the lien expires, or when the homeowner finally pays his or her dues. This is why securely keeping your documents is crucial. Once the property's back taxes are completely paid off, you will then proceed to collect all your dues. Your final payment will include your initial investments, all interests accruing, as well as any penalties due.

Should the homeowner fail to pay their property taxes on time and the tax lien expires, then you will have to seize the property immediately. The law requires that the liens and interests have to be paid in full before, or at the expiration of the lien. If not, then the property legally becomes yours. You will be at liberty to begin the eviction process, and the local sheriff's office will be able to assist here.

You can also attend tax lien auctions, which can happen across some states. In these states, the authorities often seize and auction properties where liens have expired, unpaid. These are often conducted by the county's tax office or sometimes even the sheriff's department. If you attend an auction, then you will be required to pay a certain amount of money. You will also be expected, if you place a winning bid, to pay at least 10% of the total amount, and the remaining amount within a period of 10 to 30 days. If you acquire a home through an auction or lien, renovate it and then sell it off for a profit. There are plenty of willing buyers out there looking for a good deal, so you will very likely find a buyer for the property.

Chapter 4: Property Evaluation, Bidding, and Auction

By now, you know that tax lien investing is lucrative because of certain favorable factors. One of these is that tax liens are not exposed to volatility and price fluctuations like the stock market. Also, the interest rates offered are far higher than the current low interest rates. These and other factors make tax liens the investment vehicle of choice for a lot of investors. However, there are a couple of due diligence steps that have to be followed.

As an investor, you should actually be there during the bidding process, and you should be able to evaluate properties as required. Tax lien certificates are often auctioned off by the relevant authorities to interested bidders. Highest bidders are usually those who agree on the lowest interest rates. You can purchase tax liens for only a couple of hundred dollars for some properties. Here is the best approach to follow.

Tax Lien Certificate Buying Procedures

Count the costs

Purchasing a lien is completely different from purchasing real property. As an investor, when you invest in a lien, you essentially sign up to pay all the unpaid property taxes. However, you will be the next in line to purchase the property should it come to that. Even then, it is your responsibility to ensure that the property is in such great condition that you can make good returns from it. Also, keep in mind that there are some additional costs to the lien, including certain fees and tax payments. These have to be paid up front.

Verify the lien

You will need to verify the lien on a property before buying. The reason is that some liens contain wrong information, such as the wrong address, and so on. Also, you need to collect enough data on a property, like the property's value, taxes owed, the name of the owner, and so on. You will need this information especially if the property owner files for bankruptcy, or if you perhaps discover that the property is government-owned. Things could head south if you buy a lien and then additional information surfaces. For instance, if the owner makes part payment of their back taxes or perhaps files for bankruptcy, then the lien will become invalid.

Examine and inspect the property

You should inspect a property before buying a lien. This way, you will be able to determine whether the property is worth investing in, and if the amount charged is worth the lien. There are cases where properties lose value because of certain factors such as general neglect, industrial chemicals pollution, and even natural disasters like storms. An on-site inspection is advisable because of zoning laws that determine the kind of businesses that can be set up in a certain area.

Read the local laws

Tax liens and their eventual sales are governed by laws, and each jurisdiction has its own laws and regulations. As such, you need to with the local agencies as well as state authorities to find out what laws and regulations apply to tax liens locally. Sometimes, laws vary from state to state, so reading up and confirming all laws pertaining to a particular jurisdiction is useful.

Take the example of the state of New Jersey. Tax lien holders in the state have the right to be compensated first, should the property be foreclosed. In other states such as Arizona, you will be expected to pay all subsequent taxes on a property after buying a lien. If you fail to do so, then the lien will be sold to another investor. This is why it is crucial to read about local laws in each jurisdiction from where you wish to buy liens.

Procedures for Identifying Tax Lien Properties

As noted earlier, each state has its own rules and regulations on how to handle tax liens. Even then, the basics are always similar. First, you will need to register early enough if you want to participate in tax lien auctions. Therefore, determine the state, county or city where you wish to participate as an investor, and then register as soon as possible.

As soon as your registration is complete and verified, you will have to undertake some research on the intended tax lien. Basically, there is much more than just the value of a home. There are renovations and other works that go into a home: Potential for rental property, ease of resale and so much more. This just goes to show how crucial proper research is. As such, you need to follow the procedure listed below.

- Carefully read all documents and understand what each document states exactly, and whether the information contained therein is accurate and verifiable.

- Determine the current estimated value of the home. You could use the value of other homes in the area to gauge the value.

- Take the time to drive by a property and take a good look at it. Just a visual look at a property can help you have an idea of what it actually looks like.

- Only after you perform this due diligence should you then determine whether a property is worth investing in or not.

- When you finally decide that a property is worth investing in, you should then attend the auction and place your bid. Be very careful when placing bids. Most are very competitive, so avoid the trap of overpaying as you will eventually lose out.

- In case you win a bid, then you should immediately take charge of the lien as you are now officially the owner of the tax lien.

- In most cases, delinquent homeowners eventually pay their taxes, and you will receive the interest payments due to you. However, in case the property owner fails to meet their tax obligations, then you will eventually become the property owner.

How to Bid on a Tax Lien Property

Buying tax lien certificates is totally different from all other auctions. While the bidding system varies between jurisdictions, there are certain similarities. Bidding systems are dependent on certain rules and regulations governing the sale of tax liens. There are those with strict rules, while others have more flexible procedures and processes. Here are a couple of tips that will enable you to place your bids successfully.

1. Use the bid-down approach.

The bid-down method is used when investing in tax liens. Traditionally, bidders bid upwards meaning they raise the price of the bid. However, in this instance, it is advisable to bid down the interest. This way, bidders get to determine how low the interest rates get and levels they will accept when purchasing a tax lien. Remember, though, that your profit margins will depend on the interest rates, so avoid bidding too low. The bottom line as an investor is to put your money in investments that bring in a reasonable return, so bidding too low is a strategy to avoid.

2. Bid down on the ownership.

Another alternative bidding approach that you can consider is bidding down on property ownership. This is not a very advisable approach when purchasing a tax lien certificate. It only occurs in certain states such as Iowa. In this instance, the property will be valued downwards such that the eventual bid winner will receive a lower income. Remember that your income and interest will be based on the value of the property, so a lower property value means reduced income.

3. Premium Bidding

This approach in tax lien bidding is very similar to traditional bidding. The auction is held, and the eventual winner is the bidder who offers the highest premium over the lien. Premium bidding often happens in situations where a tax lien was already auctioned but found no takers. This underscores the importance of carrying out your due diligence before buying.

4. Random Selection

Some counties and municipalities prefer the random selection approach. According to the authorities in these localities, the belief is that this approach is the best for giving investors an opportunity to invest in the tax liens. Under this approach, all bidders are given a number, and the numbers are drawn together. The bidder whose number is called first and accepts the price, wins. If the bidder turns down the offer, another number will be drawn, and the process repeats in that order.

5. Off-the-Shelf Purchase

Another approach that you are likely to come across is where you get to buy tax liens directly from the tax office within a specific jurisdiction. This often occurs in cases where tax liens were auctioned but found no willing buyers. Again, before investing in such tax liens, take time to do your due diligence. Check out the property and find out if it is worth investing in.

Crucial Points to Know About Tax Lien Bidding

There are a couple of essential facts that you need to know when investing in tax liens. First is that there is often tough competition for tax liens on properties. The competition does not just come from individual investors, but also from large investors, money managers, hedge funds, and lien investment funds.

Due to the stiff competition, the rates tend to go down drastically. This can have a drastic effect on an otherwise lucrative investment opportunity. However, apart from interest rates, there are other things to look forward to.

More than just interest rates

While interest rates sometimes fall drastically, you can expect to receive additional income from penalties charged on the amount due. Sometimes, interest rates as high as 18% have been brought down to levels of almost 0% due to intense bidding by investors.

This is because they are not just hoping to earn penalty fees, but also get the sole rights should there be a subsequent tax lien on the same property at the initial 18% rate. This is something that happens in states such as New Jersey. Since liens are issued quarterly, bidders tend to forfeit interest on the initial lien, just so as to earn a full 18% on the second and other subsequent liens.

Lien investing requires patience and cash.

In some cases, you will find that you need a lot more capital to invest in tax liens than you thought. The reason is that sometimes additional liens are issued on top of existing liens. In this case, new liens take precedence over old liens. As such, investors will have to buy the new liens just so as to protect their interests in the property.

Apart from cash, you also need patience, because tax lien investing can take time. Mostly you will need to wait upwards of 4 months, or at least 120 days. You will need to invest time and money into research and due diligence. You will also have to attend auctions and bidding in person and handle the paperwork. Therefore, if you do not have a lot of time on your hands, then you may find this to be a tricky affair.

Buy tax liens closer to your home.

You should find out a home's value before investing in it. Typically, the tax bill is often 3% or less than the value of the home. However, it could be higher for undeveloped land. Knowing the value of a property is advisable before investing. A property that is closer to home is easier to view. All that you need to do is simply drive by and take a look.

You are not necessarily investing in real estate.

It is said that less than 1% of tax lien properties end up in foreclosure. Therefore, if you are looking to buy a home, then this is definitely not the right path to follow. Numerous investors have been in this business for a while, and most of them have never experienced a foreclosure or known of a homeowner who was eventually unable to repay their back taxes.

Even then, if you do this long enough, you will probably end up with a property. Landing a property will mean a lot of things, such as hiring a lawyer to oversee the transfer, and so much more.

Chapter 5: Pitfalls and Risks of Tax Lien Investing

As with every other investment, there are certain risks and pitfalls relating to tax lien investing. Fortunately, most of these risks can be minimized and in some cases, avoided altogether. As an investor or potential investor in tax liens, you need to learn about the potential pitfalls as well as risks involved, and how to avert them. This way, you will be able to invest from the point of knowledge and avoid most of these pitfalls.

Not Understanding the Sale

One reason why investors mess up is that they get confused between tax liens and tax deeds. These are two very different financial instruments issued by municipal and county governments. If you get confused from the onset by not understanding the sale, then you will most likely lose out and probably lose money in the process. You should get informed and understand more about tax liens.

Not Doing Your Homework

Some investors are unsure about exactly what they are investing in. Some do not understand exactly what they have invested in and what they can do with it. All they know is that tax liens offer attractive returns. This kind of approach is not advisable. You really need to do your homework and understand what you are buying into exactly, where you are purchasing it, and what you can do with it.

The Property Doesn't Exist, Is Damaged, or Is Worthless

Sometimes, investors bid and pay for tax liens without doing their due diligence. As such, they may end up with liens where the property does not exist, is extensively damaged, or worth close to nothing and has no value. As it is, you need to visit a property physically and inspect it. Just driving to the site and taking a good look at the property can help you determine whether it is worth investing in or not.

Bankruptcy Cases

In some cases, property owners with back taxes often file for bankruptcy. When there are taxes due, then the property can receive a lien for property taxes owing. If the owner then goes ahead and files for bankruptcy, then a judge can remove the lien and give the home back to the owner. In such instances, it will be very difficult for investors to recover their money. Therefore, always check and confirm whether a property owner has filed for bankruptcy.

Additional Taxes

Sometimes, a property may have additional taxes attached to it. For instance, a property whose owner owes both state and federal authorities back taxes could complicate the issue. There could be other outstanding taxes as well, and these could affect your tax lien. Therefore, before purchasing a tax lien, always confirm what taxes are owed and which ones are paid.

Avoid Auction Fever

Tax liens are mostly sold to investors at auctions. During the auction process, some bidders tend to get excited as they get caught up in the process. This can be dangerous because excited investors tend to overbid and this can result in a very bad deal. When you bid and win, then you will have to buy the tax liens. If you do not, then you will possibly be banned from future auctions. Always get your priorities right and follow a plan and budget that you set up initially.

Poor Follow-Through

Most states provide delinquent property owners sufficient time to pay their back taxes. As a tax lien investor, you need to find out how long this time period is. This kind of information is basically available at the local tax office, so always check with the office. They will provide you with the information that you need for a thorough follow through.

You should also be careful about time because tax liens are limited by time. All the rights awarded to you after buying a lien will expire should this time limit expire. Remember that a tax lien is not something you can invest in and then forget about it. You do need to be vigilant. When you are vigilant and keep tab on the dates, then you will be able to earn the interests and penalty amounts due to you on time and in full. You will also need to pay any future taxes because another lien may be issued on taxes owing, and the new lien will take precedence over yours.

70

Due Diligence

Carrying out due diligence can be expensive and involves so much work. You will need to travel, make phone calls, and do some research among numerous other tasks. Due diligence is crucial because it provides sufficient information necessary for making crucial decisions. Since this requires plenty of time and finances, it may be advisable to invest passively via institutional investors. It is recommended to work with investors who are members of the NTLA.

If you are to invest on your own, then make sure you conduct your due diligence extremely well. There is a lot of information that is necessary if you are to invest wisely. Do not compromise and do not skip any essential steps. Your success or otherwise could largely be dependent on how you do your due diligence.

Other Risks

You need to be familiar with a property if you are to invest in a lien confidently. This ensures that you are able to collect your money from the owner when the time comes. Also, some properties that are dilapidated or located in tough neighborhoods are not considered a good investment. But you may not know this without proper due diligence.

There are properties that have suffered from some damage due to natural or environmental reasons. For instance, homes can be damaged by hazardous or chemical materials deposited in the area. Such properties are generally undesirable, and probably unsuitable for tax lien certificate investing.

Upon receiving a lien certificate, you should know what your responsibilities are. For instance, you will need to notify the property owner about the lien certificate purchase in writing. And towards the end of the redemption period, you will need to send another reminder should payments not be received on time and in full.

Tax liens have expiration dates and do not last forever. The expiration date comes after the expiry of the redemption period. You will need to collect any unpaid monies or take other form of action before the expiry date—otherwise, you will be unable to do so afterward. Also, should the property go into foreclosure, there is a possibility of other liens on the same property being revealed. This will likely make it difficult to acquire the title.

Also, some large investors like hedge funds and banks sometimes invest in tax liens. Such investors are able to outbid individual investors. They also drive down bids and reduce profitability. This has made it difficult for individual investors to invest profitably in tax lien certificates. Fortunately, though, there are some funds that now invest in tax lien certificates, and this opens the door for novice investors who wish to venture into this sector.

Chapter 6: Investing in Tax Deeds

Tax deed investing is a little different from investing in tax lien certificates. When it comes to tax deeds, you will be investing your money directly on a property and not a lien.

Tax deeds are also sold at auctions, so investors have to place bids. If you win a particular bid or bids, then you get the right to foreclose on the property should the owner not pay their tax debt. Within the redemption period, though, you stand to earn in penalties and interest.

What Is a Tax Deed?

A tax deed is simply a legal document that awards the ownership of a property to a government entity. This happens when the owner fails to pay taxes levied on the property.

The tax deed, once issued, gives the government power to dispose of the property in order to collect taxes levied on it. The deed is then transferred to the buyer. This kind of sale is known as a tax deed sale and is usually held at an auction.

How Does the Tax Deed Process Work?

According to the law, all property owners should pay taxes. These taxes are assessed and determined by municipal governments. Once paid, they are used to fund all the services provided by the municipal government such as water and sewerage, education, construction of highways and roads, and many more. When taxes remain unpaid for a long time, the authorities can sell the property's title or deed in order to recover their taxes.

There is a legal process that the municipal government has to follow in order to obtain a tax deed. The first step is to notify the property owner. Once notified, the authorities will then apply for a tax deed and then post a notice on the property. Another posting, a public one, will also be placed.

Sale of the Property

Delinquent properties are often sold at a public auction. A minimum bid will be indicated, which is equal to the total amount of back taxes owed, as well as all other costs, fees, and penalties. Oftentimes, it is the highest bidder that gets awarded the title to the property. The winner will be expected to pay the total amount of the bid within a period of 72 hours. In case this fails, then the auction will be invalidated, andthe process is likely to start all over again.

In some states, property owners will be given additional time—even after the auction has concluded—in order to allow them to pay their taxes and other costs and rescue their property. If the owner does not pay the taxes or even the bid amount after the auction, then the highest bidder will be awarded the property deed and will be able to foreclose the property.

The Basics of Tax Deed Investing

If you are a winning bidder, you will essentially get the right to foreclose the property. This is when the owner fails to repay their taxes as well as all other fees, charges, and other related costs. During this redemption period, the owner will be allowed to make these payments while you will be earning interests and penalty charges.

In some states, property owners do not enjoy the benefit of a redemption period. As soon as an auction takes place, the winning bidder will acquire the property and will be free to foreclose it. Even then, the law provides a grace period to the owners where they get a chance to pay all taxes and associated fees and costs in order to redeem the property. Let us examine an example of how this process works.

Example, tax deed investing:

- o Value of the property
  $60,000
- o Winning bid amount
  $21,000
- o Back taxes, costs, charges
  $ 2,300
- o Amount that goes to government
  $ 2,300
- o Money paid to the property owner
  $18,700
- o Benefit to investor
  $39,000

Sometimes, there is more than one lien on a property. For instance, the property could have a mortgage and so on. The good news here is that tax foreclosures take precedence over all other liens. In other words, tax liens are always senior liens, and they are always given priority.

Other liens on a certain property as well as any mortgages will all be rendered null and void. The new property owner or investor will acquire a fresh title that has no encumbrances. The reason why things happen this way is that the law expects other lien holders and mortgage lenders to step forward and pay all delinquent taxes, fees and charges, in case they see the need to protect the property. Should the mortgage lender and other lien holders fail to pay these taxes, then the law assumes that they have waived any claim they may have made to the property.

Where to Find Tax Deed Sales and Auctions

There are varying methods of auctioning properties across the US. In some counties, there are live auctions normally undertaken at a local venue or at the county courthouse. Today, however, more and more municipalities are conducting auctions at online platforms due to efficiency and other benefits.

You can find counties and municipalities using live, traditional, onsite auctions where they sell tax deeds and tax liens. However, this is more common in smaller regional and rural municipalities. Things are different across larger towns and cities. It is advisable to check with county and municipal treasurers to find out more about auctions within their jurisdictions.

The Process of Purchasing Tax Deeds

The entire process of buying a tax deed is pretty simple, and almost anyone can learn. The most important aspect is learning how to carry out research on a property. Secondly, you should learn how to participate in auctions and finally, how to make a profit.

1. Research the property before auction day

There are lots of bidders who put their money in properties that they have never viewed. However, you should not follow this route. It is crucial that you know what you are getting yourself into, exactly. Fortunately, the resources you need can all be found online. Simply get in touch with the county's treasurer, recorder, assessor, and surveyor.

2. Pay auction deposits and fees

There are some non-refundable fees that are charged for participating in an auction. Then, there are some deposits and charges that are refundable. Find out all about these costs and make sure to pay them in full and on time.

3. Bid and participate at the auction

As soon as you establish a list of desirable properties, you should then head over to the auction. While live auctions at the county house are great, you may prefer online auctions using the designated system.

4. Understand the terminology

Auctions have certain terminology that you need to familiarize yourself with. Terms such as "bid-down interest rates" or "bid up the price" are common, so ensure that you understand them well and use them appropriately.

5. Buy the tax deed after the auction

You can also purchase tax-foreclosed properties after the auction. A lot of properties never get sold at auctions. Municipalities and councils have ways of selling these off.

You will then need to await a redemption period which grants the property owner time to repay all his or her pending taxes on the property. This redemption period can last a few months or sometimes a few years. If the property owner pays their taxes, you will be reimbursed of all your costs, as well as interests and other costs. However, when that time lapses, then you will be free to foreclose the property.

6. Profit with tax deeds

There are three ways that you can profit with your tax deed. The first is through interest. Interest rates can range from as low as 12% to about 25%, depending on the state. Deeds are backed by the municipality, so your investment is very safe.

You can also profit through penalties charges on the property owner. Apart from interest, most municipalities and councils charge a penalty for late payment and so on. These can increase your income to as high as 40%.

The other benefit is that you can acquire a property at below market price. The main reason for issuing deeds is to recover unpaid taxes. Even then, the chances of a tax deed ending up as a foreclosure are very slim.

Conclusion

Thank you for making it through to the end of this book. Let's hope it was informative and able to provide you with all of the tools you need to achieve your goals—whatever they may be.

The next step is to begin your search for profitable tax liens to invest in. If you have carefully read this book, then you understand the process of identifying profitable tax liens. You also know where to find them. Some of the best places are in municipal, city, and county government offices and websites.

As an investor, you appreciate the immense opportunity of investing with minimal and almost non-existent risks. Many investors view tax liens and deeds as situations akin to tossing a coin. In this case, you win if you get heads, and you win *even more* if you get tails. That is how attractive tax lien investing is.

You win regardless of the outcome. If the owner pays, then you earn high interest on your income. If the homeowner fails to pay, then you get an opportunity to foreclose the property and thenown it before eventually selling it off to willing buyers at market rates.

The financial markets are generally very risky, and most investors are searching for opportunities elsewhere. Not many opportunities exist where you can make as much as 18% or even 36% without even mentioning other payments such as penalty fees and so on. If you read this book and apply what it teaches and emphasizes, then you can expect your money to grow and multiply by investing in high-yield, risk-free tax liens.

Connect with us on our Facebook page

www.facebook.com/bluesourceandfriends and stay

tuned to our latest book promotions and free

giveaways.

Made in the USA
Coppell, TX
24 August 2020

34526187R00052